Ransom Neutron Stars
Best Friends
by John Townsend

Published by Ransom Publishing Ltd.
Unit 7, Brocklands Farm, West Meon, Hampshire GU32 1JN, UK
www.ransom.co.uk

ISBN   978 178591 452 2
First published in 2017
Reprinted 2018, 2019, 2022 (twice)

Copyright © 2017 Ransom Publishing Ltd.
Text copyright © 2017 Ransom Publishing Ltd.
Cover photograph copyright © Jevtic
Other photographs copyright © Empato; PeteSherrard; ColinMyersPhotography; palliki; Chris Hepburn; Jen Grantham; IQRemix (https://www.flickr.com/people/46021126@N00); sihasakprachum; fotografixx.

Every effort has been made to locate all copyright holders of material used in this book. If any errors or omissions have occurred, corrections will be made in future editions of this book.

A CIP catalogue record of this book is available from the British Library.

All rights reserved. No part of this publication may be reproduced, stored in a retrieval system, or transmitted, in any form or by any means, electronic, mechanical, photocopying, recording or otherwise, without the prior permission of the publishers.

There is a reading comprehension quiz available for this book in the popular Accelerated Reader® software system. For information about ATOS, Accelerated Reader, quiz points and reading levels please visit www.renaissance.com. Accelerated Reader, AR, the Accelerated Reader Logo, and ATOS are trademarks of Renaissance Learning, Inc. and its subsidiaries, registered common law or applied for in the U.S. and other countries. Used under license.

The right of John Townsend to be identified as the author of this Work has been asserted by him in accordance with sections 77 and 78 of the Copyright, Design and Patents Act 1988.

Best Friends

John Townsend

Bobby was the best-known dog in Scotland.

He lived 150 years ago.

You can still see Bobby today.
A statue of him is outside a church.
The church is Greyfriars Church.

Some people call him
Greyfriars Bobby.

Jock Gray was Bobby's owner.
Jock and Bobby were best friends.

Bobby never left Jock's side.

If Jock got ill, Bobby was
always there for him.

Sadly Jock died in 1858.

His funeral was in Greyfriars Church.
Bobby was at the funeral.

He watched the coffin as it went into a grave.

From that day, Bobby kept watch at his master's grave.

People thought he was waiting for Jock to wake up.

The church warden tried to shoo Bobby away, but he kept coming back.

Greyfriars churchyard

The little dog sat on Jock's grave
in the rain and in the snow.

He sat on the grave
in the summer and in the winter.

A sign said,
"No dogs in the churchyard."

So every day they chased Bobby
away.

Bobby kept coming back. He even
slept on Jock's grave at night.

People felt sorry for little Bobby, sitting alone in the rain.

They built him a shelter next to Jock's grave.

Bobby stayed at the grave for fourteen years.

He stayed there day and night.

He only left to get food. Every day the castle gun fired at midday.

Then Bobby would run off to a pub to get some food. It was the pub where he used to go with Jock.

The pub is now called Bobby's Bar

People came from far and wide to see Bobby.

Crowds watched him run off to be fed each day.

Then they saw him return to the grave to sit by his master.

Bobby died in 1872. He was sixteen years old.

Bobby's grave is not far from his master's.

On the headstone it says:

> *"Greyfriars Bobby
> died 14th January 1872.*
>
> *Let his loyalty be a lesson to us all."*

There are other stories like this one.

Hachiko was a dog in Japan. He lived 90 years ago.

Every day Hachiko met his master at the train station in Tokyo.

Tokyo train station today

Hachiko's owner died in 1925.

For the next ten years, the faithful dog went back to the station. He greeted the four o'clock train every day.

Every day he hoped to meet his master one more time.

There is a statue of Hachiko at Tokyo train station

In 2014 a dog called Masha made the news.

Masha lived in Russia. Her owner was ill and went to hospital.

Masha stayed at home to guard his house.

Each day Masha went to visit her owner in hospital.

She would go to the hospital at the same time every day.

Sadly, Masha's owner died.

Masha didn't give up. Still she went to the hospital to visit his bed in the ward.

A doctor said, "You see her eyes – they are so sad."

A family tried to adopt Masha.

She ran away and went back to the hospital.

Now Masha lives in the hospital. The nurses and the visitors look after her.

No wonder they say,
"A dog is man's best friend of all."

Have you read?

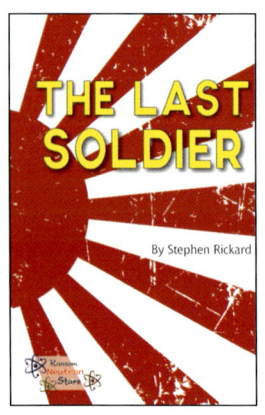

The Last Soldier

by Stephen Rickard

Text Me

by Alice Hemming

Have you read?

The Care Home

by Alice Hemming

How to Start Your Own Crazy Cult

by Stephen Rickard

Ransom Neutron Stars

Best Friends
Word count **506**

Orange Book Band

Phonics

Phonics 1	Not Pop, Not Rock Go to the Laptop Man Gus and the Tin of Ham	*Phonics 2*	Deep in the Dark Woods Night Combat Ben's Jerk Chicken Van
Phonics 3	GBH Steel Pan Traffic Jam Platform 7	*Phonics 4*	The Rock Show Gaps in the Brain New Kinds of Energy

Book bands

Pink	Curry! Free Runners My Toys	*Red*	Shopping with Zombies Into the Scanner Planting My Garden
Yellow	Fit for Love The Lottery Ticket In the Stars	*Blue*	Awesome ATAs Wolves The Giant Jigsaw
Green	Fly, May FLY! How to Start Your Own Crazy Cult The Care Home	*Orange*	Text Me The Last Soldier **Best Friends**